What's after Life?

What's after Life?

EVIDENCE FROM THE *NEW YORK TIMES*
BESTSELLING BOOK *IMAGINE HEAVEN*

JOHN BURKE

BakerBooks

a division of Baker Publishing Group
Grand Rapids, Michigan

© 2019 by John Burke

Published by Baker Books
a division of Baker Publishing Group
PO Box 6287, Grand Rapids, MI 49516-6287
www.bakerbooks.com

Printed in the United States of America

Library of Congress Cataloging-in-Publication Data
Names: Burke, John, 1963– author. | Burke, John, 1963- Imagine heaven.
Title: What's after life? : evidence from the New York Times bestselling book
    Imagine heaven / John Burke.
Description: Grand Rapids, Michigan : Baker Books, a division of Baker Group,
    [2020] | "Excerpts of this book have been taken from Imagine Heaven." |
    Includes bibliographical references.
Identifiers: LCCN 2019035114 | ISBN 9780801094637
Subjects: LCSH: Heaven—Christianity. | Future life—Christianity. | Near-
    death experiences—Religious aspects—Christianity.
Classification: LCC BT848 .B782 2020 | DDC 236/.24—dc23
LC record available at https://lccn.loc.gov/2019035114

A Global Phenomena

In London, England, a single mom was admitted to Memorial Hospital with severe bleeding.

As the blood drained from my body so did my will to live. I heard a "pop" sound and suddenly the pain stopped. . . . I had a very clear view of my body as they ferociously worked on me, hooking up a transfusion and other tubes. I recalled thinking that I just wished they would stop. I looked horrible and my color was very bad. . . . The fact that I was having these thoughts from within inches of the ceiling didn't bother me or confuse me. . . . I was totally conscious even though I had heard a nurse, the only one in a blue smock, tell the doctors I had lost consciousness soon after entering the emergency room. I was very aware of every detail of the events and the room. I was aware of a tunnel which appeared suddenly, and I was being pulled into it. I was happy to be away from that tense scene below. I floated toward the tunnel and passed right through a ceiling fan and then the ceiling. The blackness of the tunnel was churning and I began to gather speed. I was curious about my present body or form and looked at my arms and hands. They seemed to be expanding and emitting a slight glow. I felt a rush of air and a low droning noise like a vibration as I gained speed heading for a bright light far in the distance. As I proceeded at a faster rate, I felt there was a presence with me that kept me calm and emitted both love and wisdom. I didn't see anyone, but I felt the essence of my grandpa who had died when I was 13. . . . I finally came to the end and floated into a place which was overwhelmed by a radiant white light that seemed to embody all the concepts of love. A love which was unconditional and like a mother has for a child. . . . I left parochial school at 17, feeling that I had been released from an unyielding prison and was far from religious, but I knew in my heart that this was God. Words can't describe my awe in this presence. . . . I could tell He knew my every thought and feeling. The next thing I knew I was seeing a sleeping baby I knew to be me. I watched with fascination as I saw the highlights of each stage of my life. . . . I felt every good or bad deed I had ever done and its consequences upon others. It was a difficult time for me, but I was supported by unconditional love and weathered the painful parts. I was asked telepathically about whether I wanted to stay or return. . . . Suddenly, I was popped back into my body and searing pain tore through my lower body. The same nurse in the blue smock was giving me a shot and telling me to relax that the pain medication would soon begin to take affect. It seemed as if I had not been unconscious for more than a few minutes yet my visit to the "Other Side" seemed to last hours. While out of my body in the E. R., I noticed a red label on the side of the blade of a ceiling fan facing the top of the ceiling. . . . I asked if someone would please listen to my incredible experience and was told that they had no time. . . . Only one nurse in the hospital listened to me. She did so after I told her a few details of what she had said to the doctors and nurses while I was unconscious. She told of hearing of others who had been brought back from the brink of death, with similar tales. I finally convinced her to get a tall ladder and see for herself the red sticker whose appearance I described in great detail on the hidden side of the emergency room ceiling fan. The nurse and an orderly saw the sticker, confirming all the details of its appearance I described.[1]

Sounds like a fantastic, wishful fairy tale or some sort of hallucination, yet this British mom is not alone. People from around the world claim similar hard-to-believe stories after experiencing medical miracles of resuscitation. Can we just dismiss such a widespread, global phenomena that many skeptical doctors have found scientifically convincing?

In one of Europe's most prestigious medical journals, *The Lancet*, an account was reported of a patient who had experienced cardiac arrest and was brought into a Holland hospital comatose and not breathing. As a tube was placed in the patient's airway in order to ventilate him, the medical staff noted that the patient wore upper dentures. The dentures were removed and tucked into the drawer of a nearby crash cart while the patient was in a deep coma. After resuscitation, the patient was moved to another room where he remained unconscious. A week later, the patient regained consciousness. When the nurse came in, he exclaimed, "Oh, that nurse knows where my dentures are." The nurse was very surprised as the patient explained: "Yes, you were there when I was brought into the hospital and you took my dentures out of my mouth and put them onto that cart. It had all these bottles on it and there was this sliding drawer underneath and there you put my teeth." The patient claimed he had left his body and was observing the resuscitation from up near the ceiling, yet he still felt very conscious throughout the procedures. They found his lost dentures right where he said they would.[2]

In another amazing story, a woman named Simran was in an accident while traveling by bus from Mumbai, India, on the sunny morning of May 18, 2007.

All I can remember is hearing concerned voices around me all pleading with me lovingly, saying "Wake up! Wake up!" . . . I saw that the bus I was travelling on had been involved in a terrible accident, killing the bus driver and injuring many of us passengers. . . . Then I saw my blood soaked body covered with splinters. My leg was crushed badly. I fell unconscious. I opened my eyes, gasping for breath and saw myself amidst the doctors. I tried to make a sign to alert them to help me breathe. I saw the doctors and nurses cutting my clothes off. I tried to protect myself but gave up. Then a bright light appeared which had a soft male voice. It said, "You will leave everything behind. Your loved ones, the hard-earned awards, money, even your clothes. You will come to me empty handed." The light also gave me an important message and [told me] to remember it. . . . The accident rendered me disabled to this day. When people see me smiling, they wonder why I have a glow on my face. It is the glow of God. I feel very homesick and feel a sense of not belonging to this world. For I know this is not my home. . . . I have to live this life and obey the message until He calls me back. He only had love for me. It is very hard, but I am trying my best to spread the LOVE and PEACE God has for all of us.[3]

Dr. Mary Neal, an orthopedic spine surgeon, was on a white-water kayaking trip in Chile when she plunged over a waterfall. The nose of her kayak lodged between two boulders, trapping her beneath a cascading torrent of water. Dr. Neal and her boat were completely submerged under ten feet of rapids. "I very quickly knew that I would likely die,"[4] she told me when I interviewed her about her near-death experience. She could feel the intense pressure of the water as she lay bent over the front of the kayak, her bones breaking and her ligaments tearing, yet she didn't panic. Dr. Neal recalls, "At that point I completely surrendered the outcome to God's will."[5] She immediately felt physically held and reassured that everything would be fine, despite the fact that she was facing her greatest fear.

> I grew up in the water. I grew up swimming, boating, doing everything in the water, and I love the water still but I'd always, always feared a drowning death . . . but at no point did I ever have fear. I never felt air hunger. I never felt panic. I'm a spine surgeon. I certainly tried to do those things that would free me or free the boat, but I felt great. I felt more alive than I've ever felt.[6]

Dr. Neal claims her body was trapped under water for fifteen minutes, and her friends confirm she was "dead" for thirty minutes. Despite these facts, she felt alive and well the entire time, even watching their resuscitation attempts from a vantage point up above the water where she was surrounded by a celebration of people welcoming her to Heaven.

According to the *New York Times*, in 1982, "a Gallup poll reported that 8 million people have had near-death episodes" like the ones you just read.[7] What do we make of these tales of life beyond death, and how did all this get started? These global, modern-medical phenomena called near-death experiences were not widely known or often talked about; that is, until George Ritchie.

The Near-Death Experience Discovered

It was 1943 in Camp Barkley, Texas, and George Ritchie had enlisted to fight the Nazis. In the middle of boot camp, he got word that the Army would send him to medical school—his dream come true! The weather and training took their toll, and Ritchie got double pneumonia the week he was supposed to ship out to Richmond for school. The morning he'd planned to catch the train, he woke up at midnight in a sweat, heart pounding like a jackhammer, with a 106-degree fever. During X-rays, he passed out.

Where was I? Ritchie pondered.

And how had I gotten there?

I thought back trying to remember. The X-ray machine—that's right! They had taken me to the X-ray department and . . . and I must have fainted or something.

The train! I would miss the train! I jumped out of bed in alarm, looking for my clothes. . . .

I turned around, then froze.

Someone was lying in that bed.

I took a step closer. He was quite a young man, with short brown hair, lying very still. But, [this] was impossible! I myself had just gotten out of that bed! For a moment I wrestled with the mystery of [the man in my bed]. It was too strange to think about—and anyway I did not have time.

Ritchie realized the man in the bed was wearing his ring. *I must be dead!* he thought. At that moment, the light in the room started to grow brighter and brighter.

I stared in astonishment as the brightness increased, coming from nowhere, seeming to shine everywhere at once. . . . It was impossibly bright: it was like a million welders' lamps all blazing at once. And right in the middle of my amazement came a prosaic thought, probably born of some biology lecture back at the university: "I'm glad I don't have physical eyes at this moment," I thought. "This light would destroy the retina in a tenth of a second."

No, I corrected myself, not the light.

He.

He would be too bright to look at. For now I saw that it was not light but a Man who had entered the room, or rather, a Man made out of light. . . .

The instant I perceived Him, a command formed itself in my mind. "Stand up!" The words came from inside me, yet they had an authority my mere thoughts had never had. I got to my feet, and as I did came the stupendous certainty: You are in the presence of *the* Son of God.

Ritchie thought about Jesus, the Son of God, whom he had learned about in Sunday school. "Gentle, meek, kind of a weakling" was Ritchie's impression. But this person was Power itself fused together with an unconditional love that overwhelmed him.

An astonishing love. A love beyond my wildest imagining. This love knew every unlovable thing about me—the quarrels with my stepmother, my explosive temper, the sex thoughts I could never control, every mean, selfish thought and action since the day I was born—and accepted and loved me just the same.

When I say He knew everything about me, this was simply an observable fact. For into that room along with His radiant presence—simultaneously, though in telling about it I have to describe them one by one—had also entered every single episode of my entire life. Everything that had ever happened to me was simply there, in full view, contemporary and current, all seemingly taking place at that moment.

How this was possible I did not know. . . .

What have you done with your life to show Me? . . .

The question, like everything else proceeding from Him, had to do with love. How much have you loved with your life? Have you loved others as I am loving you? Totally? Unconditionally?

. . . Why, I had not known love like this was possible. Someone should have told me, I thought indignantly! A fine time to discover what life was all about. . . .

I did tell you.

But how? Still wanting to justify myself. How could He have told me and I not have heard?

I told you by the life I lived. I told you by the death I died. And, if you keep your eyes on Me, you will see more.[8]

Ritchie did see much, much more. Beauty surpassing anything he could have imagined. After being clinically dead for nine minutes, he found himself back in his earthly body, but with a sheet over his head. Dr. Francy signed a notarized statement of his death that George would later produce whenever he talked about his experience.[9] In his book, *Return from Tomorrow*, Ritchie says, "I have no idea what the next life will be like. Whatever I saw was only—from the doorway, so to speak. But it was enough to convince me totally of two things from that moment on. One, that our consciousness does not cease with physical death—that it becomes in fact keener and more aware than ever. And two, that how we spend our time on earth, the kind of relationships we build, is vastly, infinitely more important than we can know."[10]

The Common Experience

After this life-altering experience, Ritchie finally made it to medical school, worked for thirteen years as a doctor, and eventually formed what would be the precursor to the Peace Corps. At age forty, he earned his doctorate in psychiatry. Years later, Dr. Raymond Moody heard Ritchie lecture about his experience at the University of Virginia. Moody had never heard of such a thing, but he had studied Plato's works on immortality while getting his PhD in philosophy.

Moody began having his philosophy students read theories on postmortem survival and found to his amazement that about one out of every thirty students reported something similar to Ritchie's story. Moody started "collecting" these accounts, and in 1975, he coined the term "near-death experience" (NDE), publishing his findings in the international bestseller *Life after Life*. Moody said, "My hope for this book is that it will draw attention to a phenomenon which is at once very widespread and very well hidden."[11]

Moody had interviewed hundreds of people who had stories of an NDE. While no two stories were identical, many shared common core traits.

> A man is dying and, as he reaches the point of greatest physical distress, he hears himself pronounced dead by his doctor. . . . He suddenly finds himself outside of his own physical body, but still in the immediate physical environment, and he sees his own body from a distance, as though he is a spectator. He watches the resuscitation attempt from his unusual vantage point. . . . He notices that he still has a "body," but one of a very different nature and with very different powers from the physical body he has left behind. Soon other things begin to happen. Others come to meet and to help him. He glimpses the spirits of relatives and friends who have already died, and a loving, warm spirit of a kind he has never encountered before—a being of light—appears before him. This being asks him a question, nonverbally, to make him evaluate his

life and helps him along by showing him a panoramic, instantaneous playback of the major events of his life. At some point he finds himself approaching some sort of barrier or border, apparently representing the limit between earthly life and the next life. Yet, he finds that he must go back to the earth, that the time for his death has not yet come. At this point he resists ... and does not want to return. He's overwhelmed by intense feelings of joy, love, and peace. Despite his attitude, though, he somehow reunites with his physical body and lives.[12]

In the many years since Moody coined the term, studies in the United States and Germany have suggested that approximately 4.2% of the population has reported an NDE. That's one out of every twenty-five people, or nearly 13 million Americans![13]

Many other books have been written about NDEs, and careful scientific study has been done to collect stories from cultures around the world. Could people make up stories or fabricate details? Yes. For this reason, in the book *Imagine Heaven*, on which this booklet is based, I tried to choose stories from people with little to no profit motive: orthopedic surgeons, commercial airline pilots, bank presidents, professors, neurosurgeons— people who probably don't need the money but have credibility to lose by making up wild tales. I've also included children; people from predominately Muslim, Hindu, and Buddhist countries; and many people who did not write books. Amazingly, after studying over a thousand NDEs, I found that they all add color to a similar, grand picture of the afterlife. And that's my main motive in writing this booklet—to help you imagine heaven so you'll see how wise it is to live for it, plan for it, and live with no fear because you're prepared for a safe arrival someday.

Across cultures, our most common shared trait is death. The way you think about what's to come after this life affects everything—how you prioritize love, how willing you are to sacrifice for the long term, how you view suffering, what you fear or don't fear. I began studying this topic when my dad was dying. A friend gave us a copy of Dr. Moody's book. As a skeptical agnostic, it intrigued me that modern medicine could give us insight into the most important question of humanity: *What's after life?* Over the past thirty years, I've gone from a career in engineering to devoting my life to study and teach what I've learned about this life and the life to come. I've studied the Bible, the major world religions, philosophy, and over a thousand NDEs from around the world. I've concluded that the core common elements of NDEs point to something far more real than most people have ever imagined. I hope you'll travel these pages with an open mind, no matter your spiritual background, because I'm convinced your Creator loves you more than you can imagine! But why should you believe me?

What Convinced So Many Skeptical Doctors?

"I've never seen anything, no light, no shadows, no nothing," a blind woman named Vicki explained to Kenneth Ring, a professor at the University of Connecticut who was conducting a study on NDEs of blind people. Both of Vicki's optic nerves were so severely damaged that she had never visually seen anything during her twenty-two years of life. As Vicki explained, "A lot of people ask me if I see black. No, I don't see black. I don't see anything at all. And in my dreams I don't see any visual impressions. It's just taste, touch, sound, and smell. But no visual impressions of anything."[14]

That is until one fateful night when Vicki was hurled from a van and suffered a basal skull fracture and a broken back and neck. Vicki describes an NDE with its own unique elements but essentially the same contours as Dr. George Ritchie's. The testimonies of blind people like Vicki have convinced many skeptical doctors and researchers that life continues after death. Blind people somehow "see" the same elements during an NDE that sighted people see.

As Dutch cardiologist and researcher Dr. Pim van Lommel explains, the stories of Vicki and other blind people with an NDE are forcing scientists to consider new ideas about the relationship between consciousness and the brain. As Dr. van Lommel says, "Vicki's reported observations could not have been the product of sensory perception or of a functioning (visual) cerebral cortex, nor could they have been a figment of the imagination given their verifiable aspects."[15]

Kenneth Ring points out several "visual" descriptions Vicki made. For example, in her life review, Vicki "saw" a playback of her earthly life with her two friends, Debby and Diane. She was later able to describe how her childhood friends looked and even walked (one moved with great difficulty). These were observations looking back on her childhood friends that Vicki could not have seen at the time but she claimed to "see" in the life review. The researchers confirmed the observations with the housemother who raised all three girls.

In Ring's study, he interviewed twenty-one blind people (fourteen had been blind from birth) who reported an NDE. He subjected his research to peer review, and "the reviewers tended to agree on the main conclusions of the researchers, that (1) the near-death experience is the same for sighted persons and blind or vision impaired persons, (2) blind and visually impaired descriptions of the experience show visual, or 'visual-like' perceptions, and (3) some of these reports have been validated by outside witnesses. So (4) there is preliminary evidence that the visual information can be corroborated."[16]

In addition, Dr. van Lommel observed that "current scientific knowledge also fails to explain how the many NDE elements can be experienced at a moment when, in many people who report them, brain function has been seriously impaired. . . . [Also] there is no explanation for the fact that people across all ages and cultures have reported essentially similar experiences."[17]

Skeptical medical doctors became some of the first NDE researchers after *Life after Life* was published. Dr. Michael Sabom is a cardiologist who told me he heard a presentation on Moody's book but thought it was nonsense. None of the patients he'd resuscitated had ever conveyed such an imaginative story. Challenged by the presenter to actually ask his patients, he did. During five years of research, he discovered hundreds of stories.

What convinced Dr. Sabom and other skeptical doctors of life beyond death were patients claiming they had left their physical body and observed their own resuscitation. Here was corroborative evidence—some verifiable way to substantiate whether these tales were more than hallucinations or reactions of a dying brain. Dr. Sabom has recorded multiple stories like that of Pete Morton.

[Pete] told me he had left his body during his first cardiac arrest and had watched the resuscitation. When I asked him to tell me what exactly he saw, he described the resuscitation with such detail and accuracy that I could have later used the tape to teach physicians. Pete remembered seeing a doctor's first attempt to restore his heartbeat. "He struck me. And I mean he really whacked me. He came back with his fist from way behind his head and he hit me right in the center of my chest." Pete remembered them inserting a needle into his chest in a procedure that he said looked like "one of those Aztec Indian rituals where they take the virgin's heart out." He even remembered thinking that when they shocked him they gave him too much voltage. "Man, my body jumped about two feet off the table."

"Before talking with Pete, and scores like him," Dr. Sabom said, "I didn't believe there was such a thing as a near-death experience. . . . These people, like Pete Morton, saw details of their resuscitation that they could not otherwise have seen. One patient noticed the physician who failed to wear scuffs over his white, patent-leather shoes during open-heart surgery. In many cases I was able to confirm the patient's testimony with medical records and with hospital staff."[18]

Dr. Sabom published his research in *Recollections of Death* and in the *Journal of the American Medical Association* (JAMA). Dr. Jeff Long, a radiation oncologist, read the JAMA article and thought it was ridiculous. Yet as he began asking more of his resuscitated patients if they had experienced an NDE, he too discovered similar accounts. Dr. Long says, "I remember thinking these experiences could change my views about life, death, God, and the world we live in."[19] Since then, Dr. Long has collected over 4,500 NDEs in thirty-three languages from around the world. His extensive scientific study led him to conclude: "NDEs provide such powerful scientific evidence that it is reasonable to accept the existence of an afterlife."[20]

Researcher Steve Miller notes the amount of scholarly, peer-reviewed literature now available since Moody wrote *Life after Life*: "Over 900 articles on NDEs were published in scholarly literature prior to 2011, gracing the pages of such varied journals as *Psychiatry, The Lancet, Critical Care Quarterly, The Journal for Near-Death Studies, American Journal of Psychiatry, British Journal of Psychology, Resuscitation* and *Neurology*."[21] *The Handbook of Near-Death Experiences* chronicles fifty-five researchers or teams who have published at least sixty-five studies of over 3,500 NDEs.[22]

Alternative Explanations

Multiple alternative explanations have been proposed over the years. Dr. van Lommel has studied each of these possible explanations for some or all of the NDE experiences: oxygen deficiency (the fighter-pilot syndrome); carbon dioxide overload; chemical reactions in the brain; psychedelics (DMT, LSD, Psilocybin, and Mescaline); electrical activity of the brain (epileptic seizures and electrode brain stimulation); fear of death; depersonalization; dissociation; fantasy and imagination; deceit; memory of birth; hallucinations; dreams; and delusion brought on by medication.

After discussing the merits and problems of each of these alternative hypotheses, Dr. van Lommel has concluded: "The theories on NDE set out above fail to explain the experience of an enhanced consciousness, with lucid thoughts, emotions, memories from earliest child-

hood, visions of the future, and the possibility of perception from a position outside and above the body. . . .
There appears to be an inverse relationship between the
clarity of consciousness and the loss of brain function."[23]

Some skeptics claim that these patients must be "pick-
ing up" what is said or heard while they are unconscious,
but cases like that of well-known singer-songwriter Pam
Reynolds prove otherwise.

Pam Reynolds, a thirty-five-year-old mother, under-
went a complex surgery to repair a giant aneurysm in
a cerebral artery. As reported by cardiologist Michael
Sabom and neurosurgeon Robert Spetzler, in prepara-
tion for the surgery they lowered her body tempera-
ture to about 50 degrees Fahrenheit and drained all
the blood from her head, so that her brain had ceased
functioning by all three clinical tests—"her electro-
encephalogram was silent, her brain-stem response
was absent, and no blood flowed through her brain. . . ."

Additionally, her eyes were taped shut, she was
put under deep anesthesia, brain-stem activity was
monitored with "100-decibel clicks emitted by small
molded speakers inserted into her ears" and her entire
body, except for the small area of the head they were
cutting on, was covered completely.

During this time, Reynolds experienced a vivid NDE
where she watched part of the surgery and reported

back to the doctors what she saw—describing in minute detail the specialized instruments they used for the surgery. For example, she described the saw as looking "a lot more like a drill than a saw. It even had little bits that were kept in this case that looked like the case that my father stored his socket wrenches in when I was a child. . . . And I distinctly remember a female voice saying: 'We have a problem. Her arteries are too small.' And then a male voice: 'Try the other side.'" Doctors Sabom and Spetzler (director of the Barrow Neurological Institute) confirmed the accuracy of what she both heard and saw in the operating room.[24]

The fact that people across all ages and cultures have reported similar experiences is better explained by the simple conclusion: there is life after death. But what will that life be like? Every NDE is unique, and each should be filtered with a measure of skepticism. However, when thousands of people of all ages across the globe report the same core elements, we need to consider what that means for us.

The Core Elements of a Near-Death Experience

Although no two experiences are identical, there are amazingly common elements to the core NDE described by people of all ages and backgrounds. Dr. Jeff Long reports on the percentage of each core element described in his study of 1,300 NDEs from around the world.

1. Out-of-body experience: separation of consciousness from the physical body (75.4%)

2. Heightened senses (74.4% said "more conscious and alert than normal")

3. Intense and generally positive emotions or feelings (76.2% "incredible peace")

4. Passing into or through a tunnel (33.8%)

5. Encountering a mystical or brilliant light (64.6%)

6. Encountering other beings, either mystical beings or deceased relatives or friends (57.3%)

7. A sense of alteration of time or space (60.5%)

8. Life review (22.2%)

9. Encountering unworldly ("heavenly") realms (52.2%)

10. Encountering or learning special knowledge (56%)

11. Encountering a boundary or barrier (31%)

12. A return to the body (58.5% were aware of a decision to return)[25]

After thirty years of research as a practicing oncologist skeptically looking at all alternative explanations, Dr. Long concludes: "With a flat EEG [no recorded brain activity] . . . there is no chance that electrical activity in [the] lower parts of the brain could account for such a highly lucid and ordered experience as described by NDErs. Lucidity coupled with the predictable order of elements establishes that NDEs are not dreams or hallucinations, nor are they due to any other causes of impaired brain functioning."[26]

Most people who report NDEs mention that it is nearly impossible to put into words what they have experienced. So every NDE is actually an interpretation of an experience that's beyond our 3-dimensional, finite, earthly language.

Imagine that your life is like a black-and-white, 2-dimensional painting on a wall. When you die, you're "ripped" off that flat painting and brought into the 3-D room of color that was always around you but just beyond your limited 2-D perception. Now imagine going back to that flat, black-and-white existence and trying to explain what the 3-D, colorful room you were in was like—but in 2-D, black–and–white language. That's what NDErs say it's like trying to describe the extra-dimensional reality of Heaven. That's also why people who report NDEs naturally filter the experience through the grid of their beliefs.

NDErs can't actually tell us what happens after full biological death, because they did not die fully—they came back to tell us what they saw. So NDErs can't tell us what happens after you cross that "border" or "boundary" so many knew they could not cross and still return. And NDErs are also not the first to report Heaven's reality. I've studied the ancient texts of the world's religions, and although many describe Heaven, I've found that the core experience of NDEs from all across the globe align best with the Bible's exhilarating picture of the life to come. Let's look at a few ways NDEs confirm what the Bible has revealed for thousands of years to give all people hope for what's to come after this life. For the rest of this booklet, we will briefly survey the experiences of people who have NDEs with a view toward helping you imagine what Heaven will be like. For the full picture, read the book *Imagine Heaven*.

An Upgraded Body

If you expect to be a disembodied ghostly soul floating around in Heaven, you're in for a wonderful surprise. That point of life you feared most—the death of your earthly body—will suddenly free you in a way you never anticipated. You'll feel alive! In fact, so alive that you will have to adjust. You will still have a body—arms, legs, fingers, and toes—but something will be different as well. An upgrade!

NDErs say ailments and impairments will be gone, and the limitations of movement in your earthbound body won't seem to apply to this upgraded spiritual body. You'll still have your senses intact; in fact, they will seem turbocharged and multiplied. But you will sense and experience everything in a way that feels more "real" and more "alive" than ever before, not with five senses, but more like fifty senses.

This new spiritual body is a promise from God. The apostle Paul, who wrote much of the New Testament, may have been reflecting on his own near-death experience, reported in Acts 14, when he explained,

> For we know that when this earthly tent we live in is taken down (that is, when we die and leave this earthly body), we will have a house in heaven, an eternal body made for us by God himself and not by human hands. We grow weary in our present bodies, and we long to put on our heavenly bodies like new clothing. For we will put on heavenly bodies; we will not be spirits without bodies. While we live in these earthly bodies, we groan and sigh, but it's not that we want to die

and get rid of these bodies that clothe us. Rather, we want to put on our new bodies so that these dying bodies will be swallowed up by life. (2 Corinthians 5:1–4 NLT)

Not only will we be free of the pains of this earthly body but we will also feel young again! Remember what it was like to have endless energy as a child? Recall the strength and stamina of those teen years? Imagine a new body that will feel even better than that!

Marv Besteman experienced that transformation first-hand. A retired bank president, Marv had surgery at the University of Michigan Medical Center to remove a rare pancreatic tumor called an insulinoma. The night of his procedure, Marv had an NDE. He said two angels took him from the hospital room to the most beautiful place imaginable. Marv recalls:

Standing in a short line of people, I observed the other thirty-five or so heavenly travelers, people of all nationalities. Some were dressed in what I thought were probably the native costumes of their lands. One man carried a baby in his arms. I saw color-bursts that lit up the sky, way beyond the northern lights I had seen once on a trip to Alaska. Simply glorious. . . . The music I heard was incomparable to anything I had ever heard before. . . . My [old] geezer body felt young and strong and fantastic. The aches and pains and limitations of age were just gone. I felt like a teenager again, only better.[27]

Fully Known and Accepted

Many of us don't feel fully known, understood, or valued—that's why we labor to prove ourselves, get people to notice us, make a name for ourselves, or try to be like someone else. But according to what people report about Heaven in their NDEs, all this gets replaced with an unbelievable clarity of who God created you to be—fully yourself, fully unique, fully loved.

We won't lose our earthly identity; it will finally be known to us fully. We won't lose our humor, our personality, our looks, our emotions, our history, or our memories. We will finally be fully ourselves—without all the confusion and wounds and lies that cloud our true identity in this life.

Believing they are worth everything to God frees many NDE survivors to live for what really matters. Moses said it thousands of years ago and Jesus reiterated it—to love God is the first and greatest purpose of life. To love others as much as we love ourselves—that's second.

Dr. van Lommel notes that many NDE survivors he's interviewed realize love is what matters most, and they "talk of attaching greater value and meaning to life and less importance to material things such as an expensive car, a big house, and a job with status or power."[28]

Hazeliene, a single mother from Singapore, experientially discovered the truth of those findings when she blacked out, hit her head, and apparently "died." She explains in English (not her native language):

> I suddenly was in the very dark tunnel going up, up, up. . . . After passing through from that very dark tunnel, it has changed to very bright light. I had seen a very bright light, I thought it was sun, but it was not. I don't have an idea where that light came from. Someone spoke to me for a while, I heard, and that voice came from that light. You know what I felt when I saw that light? When I saw that bright light, I felt that someone loves me very much (but no idea who it was). I was very overwhelmed with that bright light. And while I was there, I felt the love, and that love I never felt before. That light welcoming me very warmly and loves me very much. My words to the light before I [revived] was this: *I wanted to stay here, but I love my two kids.* When I said this, I suddenly woke up. . . . Was it true that the light was GOD? Reason why I felt very overwhelmed? Nobody love

me like that kind of love before. How I wish, my two kids and me could go there and feel that love forever.[29]

With Loved Ones

Many who have had NDEs had a "welcoming committee" there to greet them just like Jesus taught: "Use your worldly resources to benefit others and make friends. Then, when your possessions are gone, they will welcome you to an eternal home" (Luke 16:9 NLV).

Marv Besteman recalls a welcome party of close relatives, those who had spiritually influenced him, and those he spiritually encouraged. "Both of my friends were prayer warriors, and we had spent many hours praying together. I'm not sure if this is why God chose these two guys for me to see—they were significant to me and my spiritual life. Everyone I saw had been influential in shaping my life in some way."[30]

Dr. Mary Neal said she shot out of the water and was greeted by a welcoming committee bursting with light and love: "I knew they were sent to guide me across the divide of time and dimension that separates our world from God's. I also had the unspoken understanding that they were sent not only to greet me and guide me, but also to protect me during my journey."[31]

Imagine if your life on earth transitioned into the most joyous, exciting party. Deceased relatives and friends who also loved God, along with people you've loved and helped, all gather because they just can't wait to show you around Heaven. You're still you, and they're still them—those relationships don't die, they go deeper than ever into the exploration of eternity with God and each other.

Dr. Long points out that in dreams or hallucinations, usually people claim to see recently encountered *living* people. But in NDEs they claim to see *deceased* loved ones. A study of five hundred Americans and five hundred people in India found that the vast majority of the human figures seen in visions of the dying were deceased close relatives.[32]

The Most Beautiful Place Imaginable

Dale Black had always dreamed of being a commercial pilot. And by nineteen, he already had his pilot's license. But one day when he was aloft with two pilots who were mentoring him, the plane smashed into a stone edifice at 135 miles per hour, then plunged seventy feet to the ground. You can still see the *Los Angeles Times* photo of the wreckage. Only Dale survived after having an NDE. Here is just a taste of the stunning place in which he found himself.

The fragrance that permeated heaven was so gentle and sweet, I almost didn't notice it amid all there was to see and hear. But as I looked at the delicate, perfect flowers and grass, I wanted to smell them. Instantly, I was aware of a gentle aroma. As I focused, I could tell the difference between the grass and the flowers, the trees and even the air. It was all so pure and intoxicating and blended together in a sweet and satisfying scent.

In the distance stood a range of mountains, majestic in appearance, as if they reigned over the entire landscape. These were not mountains you wanted to conquer; these were mountains you wanted to revere. . . .

My eyes were next drawn to a river that stretched from the gathering area in the middle of the city to the wall. It flowed toward the wall and seemed to end there, at least from my vantage point. The river was perfectly clear with a bluish-white hue. The light didn't shine on the water but mysteriously shone within it somehow.[33]

If you've ever nursed a fear that Heaven might be an ethereal, less-than-real, cloudy place . . . think again! The language of Scripture and the words NDErs use over and over again emphasize the opposite—this current life is the fuzzy, less-than-real shadow of the brilliant, beautiful-beyond-your-wildest-dreams, solid Life you need to grab onto.

According to the Jewish Torah, Moses was instructed to pattern the tabernacle after the one God showed him, which was "a copy and shadow of what is in heaven" (Hebrews 8:5). This implies that all we love about this earth is merely a shadow of the greater Reality to come—a beautiful place made for us.

Imagine all the beauty of earth—the majestic Sierras plunging into the deep blue California coastline, the purple-and-green aspen-lined mountain valleys of Colorado, the turquoise-encircled white sand beaches of the Virgin Islands, the gorgeous jagged coastlines of Hawaii—all of it reflects the splendor of God. If that's true, then how could we ever think Heaven, where the Creator dwells, would be less beautiful than earth?

Because most people have never read the book of Revelation in the Bible, they don't realize the earthlike beauty John mentions in his vision of Heaven. It's amazing how it matches the beauty described by NDErs around the globe.

After this I saw . . . [people] from every nation and tribe and people and language. . . . They were clothed in white robes and held palm branches in their hands. . . . He will lead them to springs of life-giving water. . . . He took me in the Spirit to a great, high mountain, and he showed me the holy city, Jerusalem. . . . It shone with the glory of God. . . . Then the angel showed me a river with the water of life, clear as crystal, flowing from the throne of God and of the Lamb. It flowed down the center of the main street. On each side of the river grew a tree of life, bearing twelve crops of fruit. (Revelation 7:9, 17; 21:10; 22:1–2 NLT)

Dr. Richard Eby, a nationally recognized physician and professor, fell two stories and landed directly on his head, splitting it open. He said he was instantly in a gorgeous valley. Even though he considered himself an amateur botanist, he couldn't name all the varieties of trees and flowers he saw during his NDE.

My gaze riveted the exquisite valley in which I found myself. Forests of symmetrical trees unlike anything on earth covered the foothills on each side. I could see each branch and "leaf"—not a brown spot or dead leaf in the forest. ("No death there" includes the vegetation!) . . . They resembled somewhat the tall arbor vitae cedars of North America, but I could not identify them. The valley floor was gorgeous. Stately grasses, each blade perfect and erect, were interspersed with ultra-white, four-petalled flowers on stems two feet tall, with a touch of gold at the centers. . . .

Then I sensed a strange new feel to the stems—no moisture! I felt them carefully. Delicately smooth, yet nothing like earthly stems with their cellular watery content. Before I could ask, again I had the answer: earthly water is hydrogen and oxygen for temporary life support; here Jesus is the Living Water. In His presence nothing dies.[34]

Alive in New Dimensions

In 2008, Harvard neurosurgeon Eben Alexander was struck by a rare illness that caused his entire neocortex— the part of the brain that makes us human—to shut down. What he experienced reversed the conclusions he had formed through medical school.

As a neurosurgeon, I'd heard many stories over the years of people who had strange experiences, usually after suffering cardiac arrest: stories of traveling to mysterious, wonderful landscapes; of talking to dead relatives—even of meeting God himself. Wonderful stuff, no question. But all of it, in my opinion, was pure fantasy. . . . If you don't have a working brain, you can't be conscious. This is because the brain is the machine that produces consciousness in the first place. When the machine breaks down, consciousness stops. . . . Pull the plug and the TV goes dead. The show is over, no matter how much you might have been enjoying it. Or so I would have told you before my own brain crashed.

My experience showed me that the death of the body and the brain are not the end of consciousness, that human experience continues beyond the grave. More important, it continues under the gaze of a God who loves and cares about each one of us and about where the universe itself and all the beings within it are ultimately going. The place I went was real. Real in a way that makes the life we're living here and now completely dreamlike by comparison. . . .

Below me there was countryside. It was green, lush, and earthlike. It was earth . . . but at the same time it wasn't. . . . I was flying, passing over trees and fields, streams and waterfalls, and here and there, people. There were children, too, laughing and playing. The people sang and danced around in circles, and sometimes I'd see a dog, running and jumping among them. . . .

Meanwhile, I was in a place of clouds. Big, puffy, pink-white ones that showed up sharply against the deep blue-black sky. Higher than the clouds—immeasurably higher—flocks of transparent orbs, shimmering beings arced across the sky, leaving long, streamer-like lines behind them. Birds? Angels? . . . A sound, huge and booming like a glorious chant, came

down from above, and I wondered if the winged beings were producing it. Again thinking about it later,
it occurred to me that the joy of these creatures, as
they soared along, was such that they had to make
this noise—that if the joy didn't come out of them
this way then they would simply not otherwise be
able to contain it. . . .

How long did I reside in this world? I have no idea.
When you go to a place where there's no sense of time
as we experience it in the ordinary world, accurately
describing the way it feels is next to impossible. . . . I
saw that there are countless higher dimensions, but
that the only way to know these dimensions is to enter
and experience them directly. . . .

Because I experienced the nonlinear nature of time
in the spiritual world so intensely, I can now understand why so much writing on the spiritual dimension can seem distorted or simply nonsensical from
our earthly perspective. In the worlds above this one,
time simply doesn't behave as it does here. It's not
necessarily one-thing-after-another in those worlds.
A moment can seem like a lifetime, and one or several
lifetimes can seem like a moment.[35]

That's exactly what the Bible tells us of God's world,
where time and space are experienced in dimensions
beyond ours. "With the Lord a day is like a thousand

years, and a thousand years are like a day" (2 Peter 3:8). Imagine a world where time is no longer an enemy, where travel no longer feels bothersome, where sights and sounds, light and color, music and singing all come alive in a way that brings ecstasy to the residents of Heaven.

One of the most intriguing commonalities of NDEs is how people describe the light and colors of Heaven. Around the globe they describe a light coming out of everything, but the light is also love and life, and the colors far surpass the color spectrum of our sun. Listen to how two blind people, Vicki and Brad, describe the light of Heaven.

Brad, who was also blind from birth, experienced a clinical "death" when he was eight years old. He found himself watching someone go get help after hearing Brad struggle for air, then he shot up through a tunnel and came out on a vast meadow bathed in brilliant light.

> It seemed like everything, even the grass I had been stepping on seemed to soak in that light. It seemed like the light could actually penetrate through everything that was there, even the leaves on the trees. There was no shade, there was no need for shade. The light was actually all-encompassing. Yet I wondered how

I could know that because I had never seen before that point. . . . I felt like I wouldn't understand it had it happened on earth. But where I was, I was able to accept it almost immediately.[36]

Vicki shared a very similar experience.

Everybody there was made of light. And I was made of light. What the light conveyed was love. There was love everywhere. It was like love came from the grass, love came from the birds, love came from the trees.[37]

Later Vicki shared more of what she saw in the documentary *The Day I Died*.

It was incredible, really beautiful, and I was overwhelmed by that experience because I couldn't really imagine what light was like. It's still . . . a very emotional thing when I talk about this.[38]

Blind people would never expect light to come "out of" everything, since on earth they would hear that light shines "down on" everything. Yet around the globe, NDErs say the same things. Captain Dale Black recalls, "Somehow I knew that light and life and love were connected and interrelated. . . . Remarkably, the light didn't shine on things but through them. Through the grass.

Through the trees. Through the wall. And through the people who were gathered there."[39]

NDEs from diverse cultures reflect exactly what the Bible claims of Heaven's light: "And the city has no need of sun or moon, for the glory of God illuminates the city, and the Lamb is its light. The nations will walk in its light" (Revelation 21:23–24 NLT). And Jesus told us this light of God, who is love, will shine through the people of Heaven: "the righteous will shine like the sun in their Father's Kingdom" (Matthew 13:43 NLT).

The Being of Light

The highlight of many NDEs is a mystical Being of Light who fills them with a love beyond imagination. In Dr. Long's study, 49.9% of people said they encountered a "definite being, or voice clearly of mystical or other-worldly origin."[40] But just who is this Being of Light? Not surprisingly, this question is where researchers' opinions diverge most.

Erlendur Haraldsson and Karlis Osis, two Scandinavian researchers, studied five hundred Americans and five hundred Indians to determine how much religious or cultural conditioning shaped one's NDE. They noted, "If the patient sees a radiant man clad in white who induces in him an inexplicable experience of harmony and peace, he might interpret the apparition in various ways: as an angel, Jesus, or God; or if he is a Hindu, Krishna, Siva, or Deva."[41]

Though I have heard researchers state conclusions like this, I have never read of NDErs describing anything like Krishna (who has blue skin) or Siva (who has three eyes). Though they may have different interpretations depending on their culture, what NDErs describe is similar across cultures. People everywhere know intuitively this is God. This God is Light and Love, and in God's presence, they've never felt so known, loved, or alive. The characteristics of this God of Light reported around the world seem amazingly consistent with what the Bible reveals.

Haraldsson and Osis state that "the phenomenon within each culture often do not conform with religious afterlife beliefs. . . . Christian ideas of 'judgment,' 'salvation,' and 'redemption' were not mirrored in the visions of our American patients." I examine this claim in depth in the book *Imagine Heaven* to show how Osis and Haraldsson's expectations of these ideas do not match what the Bible teaches; however, they also note:

Several basic Hindu ideas of the afterlife were never portrayed in the visions of the Indian patients. The

various Vedic "loci" of an afterlife—Hindu Heaven—
were never mentioned. Nor were reincarnation and
dissolution in Brahma, the formless aspect of God
which is the goal of Indian spiritual striving. The
concept of Karma—accumulation of merits and
demerits—may have been vaguely suggested by reports of a "white robed man with a book of accounts."[42]

None of the Indians in Haraldsson and Osis's studies mentioned the ultimate Hindu goal of *moksha*, the
self finally absorbed into the impersonal ultimate form
of God, yet Indians did sometimes describe a loving,
personal, white-robed Being of Light with a beard and
a book of accounts. "The [Indian] patient seemed to die.
After some time, he regained consciousness. He then
told us that he was taken away by messengers in white
clothing, and brought up to a beautiful place. There he
saw a man in white, with an account book."[43]

Haraldsson and Osis say, "[In Indian NDEs], the man
with the 'book of accounts' is always pictured as a benign
ruler. An aura of sacredness rests upon him regardless of
whether he is called 'the man in a white robe' or 'God.'"[44]
Steve Miller studied western versus nonwestern NDE
accounts and discovered the same: "An Indian reported
a person with a beard, looking through books to see if
the NDEr was to remain or to be sent back." Miller says,

"I found all the common western elements in the non-western experience."[45]

These research subjects might *not* be describing their own cultural ideas of Heaven, but they *are* describing the Heaven of the Bible. The Old Testament prophet Daniel, while living in Babylon in the sixth century BCE, saw this vision of Heaven:

> As I kept looking, thrones were set up and the One Who has lived forever took His seat. His clothing was as white as snow and the hair of His head was like pure wool. His throne and its wheels were a burning fire [describing brilliant light]. . . . The Judge was seated, and The Books were opened . . . [and I] saw One like a Son of Man coming with the clouds of heaven. He came to the One Who has lived forever, and was brought before Him. And He was given power and shining-greatness, and was made King, so that all the people of every nation and language would serve Him. His rule lasts forever. It will never pass away. (Daniel 7:9–10, 13–14 NLV)

NDErs find that while this Being of Light fills them with awe, the Being also overwhelms them with an absolute love and acceptance. As one man in Moody's study put it emphatically, "I *never* wanted to leave the presence of this being." Even a mother with young children she loved more than anything said, "Now, this is the part that is hard to get across: when I had this wonderful feeling, there in the presence of that light, I really didn't want to come back. But . . . I knew that I had a duty to my family. So I decided to try to come back."[46]

Khalida, a woman from Bethlehem, described being with this Being of Light: "I was so consumed by His presence that I dropped to my knees and looked up at Him. He is so glorious, so beautiful. All light inside of Light."[47]

Samaa, a woman who grew up in the Middle East, said, "He radiated an amazing love that contained deep acceptance. I felt neither condemnation nor shame."[48]

Who Is This God of Light and Love?

The central theme of the Bible is that God wants a relationship of love with you and every person he created— love is why he created us. But love requires freedom, risk, and choice. That means God chose to subject himself to the same emotional roller-coaster ride love subjects every person to—the possibility of rejection and heartbreak.

In the Bible, God uses every relational metaphor imaginable so that we might understand how he feels about us. God poured out his heart to Jeremiah the prophet when the people he loved kept rejecting him to love and worship other things.

> "I have loved you with an everlasting love.
>> I have drawn you with unfailing
>>> kindness. . . .
> Is not Ephraim my dear son,
>> the child in whom I delight?
> Though I often speak against him,
>> I still remember him.
> Therefore my heart yearns for him;
>> I have great compassion for him,"
>>> declares the Lord. (Jeremiah 31:2, 20)

> I thought to myself,
>> "I would love to treat you as my own
>>> children!"
> I wanted nothing more than to give you this
>> beautiful land—
>> the finest possession in the world.
> I looked forward to your calling me "Father,"
>> and I wanted you never to turn from me.
> But you have been unfaithful to me.
>> (Jeremiah 3:19–20 NLT)

God loves us like a father loves a wayward child. Even though we rebel and run away, breaking his heart, God yearns to show compassion, forgive, and take us back. NDErs commonly experience two things in the presence of this God of Light: an overwhelming love and compassion and a life review where this Being emphasizes the impact of their actions on others. Researcher Steve Miller said, "In my nonwestern sample, I saw no significant difference in life reviews compared to western life reviews."[49]

Suresh, a woman from India, recalls the relational nature of her NDE: "I realized that god was love, light and motion and to be able to receive him in the heart one had to cleanse it and mind by apologizing to all people I was associated with and with whom I had differences, arguments or quarrels or all those whom I might have knowingly or unknowingly caused pain. The kind of love that I experienced there cannot be expressed in words."[50]

NDErs, regardless of culture, are acutely aware of falling short of what they know to be right. All the world's religions teach us the same basic moral law, yet we all break it. We can't even keep our own moral law. Have you ever said, "I'll never ... ," but you did? The world's religions remind us something's wrong and that we're all royal screwups! The world's a mess. We all desperately need God's help. The question is, what will God do with our moral failures?

Rene was pronounced "dead" by her neurosurgeon the day after she hydroplaned on the streets of Sydney, Australia, hitting an industrial power pole. On the way to the morgue, she was revived and was able to share her experience.

I arrived in an explosion of glorious light into a room with insubstantial walls, standing before a man about in his 30s about 6 foot tall, reddish brown shoulder length hair and an incredibly neat, short beard & moustache. He wore a simple white robe, light seemed to emanate from Him and I felt He had great age and wisdom. He welcomed me with great Love, Tranquility, Peace (indescribable), no words. I felt "I can sit at your feet forever and be content," which struck me as a strange thing to think/say/feel. I became fascinated by the fabric of His robe, trying to figure out how light could be woven!

He stood beside me and directed me to look to my left, where I was replaying my life's less complimentary moments; I relived those moments and felt not only what I had done but also the hurt I had caused. Some of the things I would have never imagined could have caused pain. I was surprised that some things I may have worried about, like shoplifting a chocolate as a child, were not there whilst casual remarks which caused hurt unknown to me at the time were counted.

When I became burdened with guilt, I was directed to other events which gave joy to others. Though I felt unworthy . . . I received great Love.[51]

Despite vividly seeing all their deeds, good and evil, NDErs do not experience a God who desires to condemn. They experience loving compassion and a willingness to forgive. Yet if you search the gods of the world's religions, how many claim to uphold justice and righteousness, record our every thought and deed, yet still extend forgiveness and loving compassion? This describes the God of the Bible, who does this all for loving relationship with us.

The Bible says God is love. He loves us like children and wants to forgive all humanity, but in order to set us free from our debts, someone has to pay to make things right. That's what Jesus said he came to do: "For God so loved the world that he gave his one and only Son, that whoever believes in him shall not perish but have eternal life. For God did not send his Son into the world to condemn the world, but to save [set right] the world through him" (John 3:16–17, brackets mine). That explains why NDErs experience compassion rather than condemnation. But why was Jesus's death necessary? If God wants to forgive us and restore our relationship, why doesn't he just forgive us? It's a reasonable question.

Imagine if you let me borrow your brand-new $85,000 sports car and asked me not to drive fast on winding roads. I knew I could handle it, so I disobeyed your will and ended up crashing and destroying your car. I'd owe you $85,000 to make things right. But what if I said to you, "Hey, why don't you *just forgive* me?" If you just forgive me the $85,000 I owe to replace your car, you are still going to have to pay for it—you'll have to pay for a new car to set things right—to make things as they were before I wronged you.

For justice to be done, someone has to pay to set things right. Either we pay the consequences of rebellion against our Creator—which is separation from God, the Source of all light, life, and love—or we recognize our need, ask his forgiveness, and he pays it for us through Jesus's death. He does this so all willing people can live free of the fear of condemnation and free of the fear of death, knowing that our Creator loves us like his own children. But love can't be forced, so God doesn't force himself on us; he lets us freely choose him.

But Jesus Was an Ordinary Man, Wasn't He?

Some might say that the Being of Light is far more impressive than Jesus was when he walked on earth. And indeed, Jesus was a normal flesh-and-blood man. But consider how Jesus appeared when he let Peter, James, and John see his glory: "As the men watched, Jesus' appearance was transformed so that his face shone like the sun, and his clothes became as white as light" (Matthew 17:2 NLT).

A Christian woman from India was resuscitated after her heart stopped in the hospital. Afterwards, she said, "I felt myself going up. There was a beautiful garden full of flowers. I was sitting there. Suddenly I felt beaming light and Jesus Christ came to me. He sat and talked to me. Light was all around."[52] That aligns with what Jesus said in John 8:12: "I am the light of the world. If you follow me, you won't have to walk in darkness, because you will have the light that leads to life" (NLT).

Ian, a young surfer in Mauritius, knew he was dying after being stung by multiple box jellyfish. In the ambulance, as he felt his life slipping away, he cried out for forgiveness, prayed the Lord's Prayer as his mother had taught him, then passed away.

> I came out of the end of the tunnel and seemed to be standing upright before the source of all the light and power. My whole vision was taken up with this incredible light. It looked like a white fire or a mountain of cut diamonds sparkling with the most indescribable brilliance. . . .

As I stood there, questions began racing through my heart; "Is this just a force, as the Buddhists say, or karma or Yin and Yang? Is this just some innate power or energy source or could there actually be someone standing in there?" I was still questioning it all.

As I thought these thoughts a voice spoke to me from the centre of the light. It was the same voice that I had heard earlier in the evening. The voice said, "Ian, do you wish to return?". . . I replied, "If I am out of my body I don't know where I am, I wish to return." The response from this person was, "If you wish to return Ian you must see in a new light."

The moment I heard the words "see in a new light," something clicked. I remembered being given a Christmas card, which said, "Jesus is the light of the world," and "God is light and there is no darkness in him." . . .

I found myself beginning to weep uncontrollably as the love became stronger and stronger. It was so clean and pure, no strings attached. . . . God showed me that when I'd asked for forgiveness in the ambulance, it was then that he forgave me and washed my spirit clean from evil. . . . This love was healing my heart and I began to understand that there is incredible hope for humankind in this love. . . .

As I stepped into the light it was as if I'd come inside veils of suspended shimmering lights, like suspended stars or diamonds giving off the most amazing

radiance. . . . Standing in the centre of the light stood
a man with dazzling white robes reaching down to his
ankles. I could see his bare feet. The garments were not
man-made fabrics but were like garments of light. As
I lifted my eyes up I could see the chest of a man with
his arms outstretched as if to welcome me.

I looked towards his face. It was so bright; it seemed
to be about ten times brighter than the light I'd already seen. It made the sun look yellow and pale in
comparison. It was so bright that I couldn't make out
the features of his face. . . . I knew that I was standing
in the presence of Almighty God—no one but God
could look like this.[53]

In the Bible, the apostle John's account of seeing Jesus
several decades after the crucifixion sounds somewhat
like a modern-day NDE.

I was exiled to the island of Patmos. . . . Suddenly, I
heard behind me a loud voice like a trumpet blast. It
said, "Write in a book everything you see. . . ."

[There] was someone like the Son of Man. He was
wearing a long robe with a gold sash across his chest.
His head and his hair were white like wool, as white
as snow. And his eyes were like flames of fire. His feet
were like polished bronze refined in a furnace, and his

voice thundered like mighty ocean waves. . . . And his face was like the sun in all its brilliance. . . .

[He] said, "Don't be afraid! I am the First and the Last. I am the living one. I died, but look—I am alive forever and ever! And I hold the keys of death and the grave." (Revelation 1:9–11, 13–18 NLT)

When we think about Jesus only as a meek, mild-mannered religious figure, stain-glassed into obscurity and mostly out of touch with our lives today, we have been deceived. Jesus revealed the almighty, all-knowing, ever-present, infinite Creator of the universe in a form we could relate to because God wants relationship. God is relatable, and he joined himself to his creation so we would love and trust him fully.

Samaa grew up in a Middle-Eastern family. She learned about Jesus from her martial arts instructor. She started attending a church, but one Sunday, the church building was ripped to shreds by a terrorist's bomb. Ten of Samaa's friends died around her, but she came back to describe meeting Jesus.

Thrown ten feet into the air and smashed against the opposite wall, I called out to Jesus silently in my agony: "Jesus, help me!" And then, in that instant, my spirit left my body and I died. . . . When I opened my eyes I saw brilliant white light illuminating Jesus, the Son of Man, the Son of God. His face was brighter than the sun, and He was so glorious. . . . It was as if Jesus could see through me, reading all the thoughts of my heart. My whole body was shaking. I felt so unworthy to be in His presence. . . . He radiated an amazing love that contained deep acceptance. I felt neither condemnation nor shame. . . .

"Welcome home, Samaa," He said in a voice sweet and gentle, yet also powerful, like the sound of many waters. He opened His arms to me. His beautiful eyes were like blazing fires of consuming love that overwhelmed me. Like a magnet, His love drew me in. . . .

"Do you want to go back or stay here in heaven?" Jesus asked. Then He showed me my life. As if seeing snapshots of a movie, I watched myself growing up. The nineteen years I'd lived passed in front of my eyes. After seeing the choices I had made, I realized I had been living for my own agenda and repented. . . . He is also a Gentleman. He never forced me but gave me the freedom to choose. As I told Him my choice—that I wanted to go back. . . .

"All right, see you soon," He said.

Immediately a fresh wave of love washed over me. It felt so easy to talk to Him, to communicate, like a child speaking to her Father.[54]

Some people seek knowledge of God after an NDE, but some don't. Some seek knowledge to re-create the experience rather than seeking God. Seeing is *not* believing. That's why having an NDE is not needed to know or love God, and in fact, most who have an NDE fight depression for having to come back. Seeing God does *not* ensure full trust of or loving faithfulness to God, and yet that's what God wants most.

Well-known atheist A. J. Ayer had a cardiac arrest and clinically died. "The only memory that I have . . . encompassing my death, is very vivid. I was confronted by a red light, exceedingly bright, and also very painful even when I turned away from it. I was aware that this light was responsible for the government of the universe. . . . I also had the motive of finding a way to extinguish the painful light."[55] God gives us freedom to choose him or to rule our own lives without him. Perhaps the loving light of the world is painful to those who reject him.

Not All Good

Not every NDE is pleasant, and we can't ignore the prevalence of these "hellish" experiences either. *The Handbook of Near-Death Experiences* reports that twelve different studies involving 1,369 subjects found that 23%

of people "reported NDEs ranging from disturbing to terrifying or despairing."[56]

Dr. Pim van Lommel summarizes hellish NDEs: "To their horror, they sometimes find themselves pulled even deeper into the profound darkness. The NDE ends in this scary atmosphere. . . . Such a terrifying NDE usually produces long-lasting emotional trauma. Not surprisingly, it is also known as a 'hell experience.' The exact number of people who experience such a frightening NDE is unknown because they often keep quiet out of shame and guilt."[57]

Are these people actually in hell? Not fully, because just like Heaven experiences, all of them came back to life. They didn't die completely. They didn't cross that border or boundary; they only tasted death. What people experience is a warning of the reality of hell.

Howard Storm, professor of art at Northern Kentucky University, was taking students on a tour of Paris's museums when a stomach ulcer perforated his duodenum. In the hospital, Howard fought to stay alive, but ultimately he passed away.

He later wrote, "I knew for certain that there was no such thing as life after death. Only simpleminded people believed in that sort of thing. I didn't believe in God, or heaven, or hell, or any other fairy tales." He expected oblivion, but instead, he found himself alive, standing in the hospital room. At first, Howard felt so wonderful he didn't realize he was dead. He encountered a "welcoming committee" of nice people he thought were hospital staff, but they deceived him and led him into an outer darkness exactly like Jesus described (see Matthew 8:11–13). There in that horrifying darkness these beings turned on him and mauled him like the worst prison scene imaginable.

> At first, it was pushing, kicking, pulling, hitting. And then that became biting and tearing with their fingernails and hands. And they were taking pieces of me and there was a lot of laughter, a lot of very foul language. And, then, they became more invasive, and I don't ever go further with this because it was so demeaning. I mean, I don't talk about it. There has never been a horror movie or a book that can begin to describe their cruelty because their cruelty was pure . . . purely sadistic. The emotional pain of what they had done to me was worse than the physical pain. The physical pain was pain from head to foot; just, solid, horrible, acute pain. On a scale of 1 to 10: 10, total. It didn't begin to match what I felt on the inside. . . . And, in that place, I heard a voice which I identified as my voice except that it did not come out of my throat. . . . It's strange but I feel like it came out of my chest. This voice said,

"Pray to God," and I thought, *I don't believe in God. I don't pray.* The voice said, "Pray to God," and I thought, *I don't even know how to pray. I couldn't pray if I wanted to pray.* The voice said, "Pray. To. God."[58]

But eventually in his desperation, Howard remembered a song he had learned when his neighbor took him to church as a child: "Jesus loves me this I know."

> I thought, *Why would [Jesus] care about me? Even if he is [real] why would he care? He must hate me. I'm so sorry.* I thought, *Enough of this! I'm done! I don't have anything else.* I wanted it to be true that Jesus loved me. . . . I yelled into the darkness, "Jesus, save me!" I have never meant anything more strongly in my life.[59]
>
> And, when I said that, I saw a light. A tiny, little speck of light and it, very rapidly, got very bright and came over me. And, I saw out of the light: hands and arms emerge out of this impossibly beautiful light . . . so intense, it's way brighter than the sun. . . . And, these hands and arms came out and they reached and they touched me and when they touched me, in that light, I could see me and all the gore. And, I was road-kill. All that gore began to just dissolve and I became whole.
>
> And, much more significantly to me than the physical healing was that I was experiencing a love that is

beyond—far beyond words. I have never been able to articulate it, but I can say that if I took all my experience of love in my entire life and could condense it into a moment, it still wouldn't begin to measure up to the intensity of this love that I was feeling. And, that love is the foundation of my life from that moment on. . . .

He just gently picked me up and held me up against him real tight, up against his chest. So, there I am: with my arms around him, his arms around me. And, I am bawling like a baby. I am slobbering and snotting and drooling with my head buried in his chest. And, he starts to rub my back, like a mom or dad with a child. And, I knew. I don't know how I knew, but I knew that he loved me very much, just the way I was. *Jesus does love me.* . . . I had called out to Jesus and he came to rescue me. I cried and cried. . . . Joy upon joy billowed through me.[60]

In the 1970s when NDE reports were increasing, few if any persons experiencing hellish NDEs came forward. In fact, Moody boldly stated, "No one has described the cartoonist's heaven of pearly gates, golden streets . . . nor a hell of flames and demons with pitchforks. So, in most cases, the reward punishment model of the afterlife is abandoned and disavowed."[61] But Moody's declaration was overcharacterized and premature. While hellish NDEs are troubling to us all, we can't ignore them.

NDErs and the Bible tell us that we are eternal be-ings, and in this life on earth we are given many, many chances to choose life instead of death eternally. God gives us small tastes of Heaven through love and beauty and creativity. But we also see warnings of hell through the evils of racism, rape, torture, genocide, and so much more suffering that comes from humans rejecting God's will and seeking their own will.

God does not want us to fear death or condemnation, but he also won't force us to love him or follow his will. Love can't be forced. It requires a choice. He has made entrance to Heaven so simple that anyone, anywhere, can call on his name. As it is revealed in Romans 10:13: "Everyone who calls on the name of the Lord will be saved." The Bible claims that Jesus's death on the cross paid for our sins against God to make this forgiveness possible. The only thing that can keep us out of Heaven is our own pride—wanting to play God and keep God out of our lives instead of seeking God's forgiveness and loving guidance.

But what will happen to those who have never heard his name? Ultimately, we don't know. But we do know God looks at the heart, he is just, and Scripture tells us it is by faith that a person is saved or set right with God forever (see Ephesians 2:8–10). God alone can judge justly, and he promises that no matter where you've been or what you've done, "if from there you seek the Lord your God, you will find him if you seek him with all your heart and with all your soul" (Deuteronomy 4:29).

The Life Review

We have seen that 22.2% of people in Dr. Long's study experienced a life review, through which they were able to assess the impact of their actions on others. According to researchers, the life review in the presence of God often has the most dramatic impact on the life of a person who has experienced an NDE. It clarifies what really matters to God, as he shows people that every action, large or small, affects others.

The majority of life reviews start with a question from the God of Light. NDErs phrase it differently, but they all hear basically the same thing: "What have you done with the life I gave you?" It's not said in judgment, but in love, to prompt reflection and learning.

God records every thought, every act, every motive. He promises to reward those who love him and have been faithful to him. Jesus reminds us what to live for: "'You must love the Lord your God with all your heart, all your soul, and all your mind.' This is the first and greatest commandment. A second is equally important:

'Love your neighbor as yourself'" (Matthew 22:37–39). And Jesus said, "The Son of Man is going to come in his Father's glory with his angels, and then he will reward each person according to what they have done" (Matthew 16:27). The life review NDErs experience seems to be a preview. It's not the judgment, but it is an opportunity to live for what truly lasts.

Regardless of cultural or religious upbringing, the life review appears consistent around the globe. People are shocked to experience not only their whole lives but even their secret thoughts and motives. After Howard Storm was rescued from outer darkness, Jesus asked him if he wished to view his life; unsure of what to expect, Howard agreed. Here's how he described his life review to me.[62]

> There are these angels in a semicircle around us. I'm being held. I'm now facing them with Jesus' arms still around me, holding me. . . . Jesus wanted them to play out, in chronological order, the scenes of my life. Mine was not as some people describe: panoramic, instantaneous. Mine was chronological from when I was born up to the present, moment by moment, life by life . . . in detail; including knowing [and] experiencing the feelings of the people that I was interacting with. . . . The entire emphasis was on my interaction

with other people—of course, initially, starting out with my mother and father, my sisters . . . school and friends.

Jesus told us that in the final day God will say, "When you loved, served, clothed, fed, cared for the least important person, you did it to me—now come and receive your reward" (Matthew 25:31–6, my paraphrase). Dr. Long observes, "Near-death experiencers generally noted that they were the ones who judged themselves."[63] This God of Light, though, offers compassion. Jesus said this would be the case: "For by your words you will be acquitted, and by your words you will be condemned" (Matthew 12:37).

Dr. Mary Neal, while trapped under water by her kayak, relived her whole life while Jesus held her.

My life was laid bare for all its good and bad. One of the things we did was look at many, many, many events throughout my life that I would have otherwise called terrible or horrible or sad or bad or tragic. And, instead of looking at an event in isolation, or looking at how it impacted me and my little world, I had the most remarkable experience of seeing the ripple effects of the event when seen 25, 30, 35 times removed . . . [and how it] changed me and changed others such that again and again and again, I was shown that in-deed, it is true: beauty comes of all things. It was really a life-changing experience.[64]

Through this experience, I was able to clearly see that every action, every decision, and every human interaction impacts the bigger world in far more significant ways than we could ever be capable of appreciating.[65]

God's love for us is not based on our good or bad deeds: it's there for us to receive as a free gift. "God saved you by his grace when you believed. And you can't take credit for this; it is a gift from God. Salvation is not a reward for the good things we have done, so none of us can boast about it" (Ephesians 2:8–9 NLT). But God does care about how we treat each other, and the life review reminds us that God will one day reward every small act of kindness and every good deed done in love for God or other people.

Every Nation, Tribe, People, and Language

We live in such a divided world, where race gets pitted against race, person against person, nation against nation. But God's plan is to unite all people in his love. It's what we all want, but without God's will and ways fully being followed, we struggle. Yet in John's vision of

Heaven, and as many NDErs proclaim, God is building a family from all nations that he will bring into perfect unity in his love.

In the last book of the Bible, in John's vision of Heaven, he sees "a vast crowd, too great to count, from every nation and tribe and people and language, standing in front of the throne and before the Lamb [Jesus]" (Revelation 7:9 NLT). Marv Besteman also saw the diversity of people that made up Heaven's community.

> The smiling people who stood in that line were from all over the world and wore all kinds of different clothing. I saw many different nationalities represented, including Scandinavian, Asian, African, and Middle Eastern . . . [as well as] primitive African tribes; they were wearing loose, flowing tribal gowns and toga-like garb with sandals on their feet.[66]

Jesus prayed that we would learn to experience more and more on earth what will happen fully in Heaven's family. He said, "I pray also for those who will believe in me through their message, that all of them may be one, Father, just as you are in me and I am in you. May they also be in us so that the world may believe that you have sent me" (John 17:20–21). In Heaven, Jesus's prayer is tangibly felt by all.

Captain Dale Black describes it well: "The best unity I have ever felt on earth did not compare with the exhilarating oneness that I experienced with my spiritual family in heaven. This love . . . God's love, was transforming."[67]

If you want a full picture of what it will be like to have a body in Heaven, to see the beauty of Paradise and the kinds of dwellings we will live in, to glimpse the heavenly city, to experience the light and colors of Heaven, to come face-to-face with the God of Light, to have enhanced senses of sight and sound, to travel with mere thought, and to be reunited with loved ones, you can find all that and more in the book *Imagine Heaven*. The stories of hundreds of people from around the world will astonish you.

Heaven will be a thriving, joyful, festive place, where families and friends work together, play together, experience real community with one another, and gather for parties to celebrate life with the Giver of Life. All the struggle, the suffering, every act of faith, service, and sacrifice done on this earth will one day be worth it. The life you always knew you were meant to live is coming. The most wonderful experiences imaginable lie before you. Imagine Heaven! Live for it now!

**TO SEE VIDEOS OF NDERS
IN THIS BOOK AND
TO EXPLORE THIS TOPIC DEEPER,
GO TO WHATSAFTERLIFE.COM.**

Notes

1. "Mary NDE," NDERF.org, accessed August 8, 2019, https://www.nderf.org/Experiences/1mary_nde.html.

2. *The Lancet* article cited in *Journal of Near-Death Studies* 27, no. 1 (Fall 2008): 48 (online reference: http://netwerknde.nl/wp-content/uploads/jndsden-tureman.pdf).

3. "Simran W NDE," NDERF.org, accessed April 29, 2015, http://www.nderf.org/NDERF/NDE_Experiences/simran_w_nde.htm.

4. From the transcript of an interview with Dr. Mary Neal by John Burke, October 2015.

5. From the transcript of an interview with Dr. Mary Neal by John Burke, October 2015.

6. From the transcript of an interview with Dr. Mary Neal by John Burke, October 2015.

7. "Near-Death Experiences Illuminate Dying Itself," *New York Times*, October 28, 1986, https://www.nytimes.com/1986/10/28/science/near-death-experiences-illuminate-dying-itself.html.

8. George G. Ritchie and Elizabeth Sherrill, *Return from Tomorrow* (Grand Rapids: Spire, 1978), 36–55. Used by permission.

9. Ritchie and Sherrill, *Return from Tomorrow*, 93.

10. Ritchie and Sherrill, *Return from Tomorrow*, 20.

11. Raymond Moody Jr., *Life after Life* (New York: HarperCollins, 2001), 5.

12. Kenneth Ring and Sharon Cooper, *Mindsight: Near-Death and Out-of-Body Experiences in the Blind* (Bloomington, IN: iUniverse, 2008), Kindle edition.

13. Pim van Lommel, *Consciousness Beyond Life: The Science of the Near-Death Experience* (New York: HarperCollins, 2010), Kindle edition, location 9.

14. British Broadcasting Company, *The Day I Died: The Mind, the Brain, and Near-Death Experiences*, film (2002), http://topdocumentaryfilms.com/day-i-died/.

15. Van Lommel, *Consciousness Beyond Life*, 26.

16. Van Lommel, *Consciousness Beyond Life*, 136.

17. Van Lommel, *Consciousness Beyond Life*, 132–33.

18. Michael Sabom, *Light and Death* (Grand Rapids: Zondervan, 2011), Kindle edition, locations 83–90, 122–25.

19. Synopsis of Sheila's NDE (including direct quotes) from Jeffrey Long and Paul Perry, *Evidence of the Afterlife: The Science of Near-Death Experiences* (New York: HarperCollins, 2009), Kindle edition, location 26–30.

20. Long and Perry, *Evidence of the Afterlife*, 44.

21. J. Steve Miller notes that *The Index to NDE Periodical Literature* collects these articles: http://iands.org/research/index-to-nde-periodical-literature.html; *Near-Death Experiences as Evidence for the Existence of God and Heaven: A Brief Introduction in Plain Language* (Acworth, GA: Wisdom Creek Press, 2012), Kindle edition, location 8.

22. J. M. Holden, B. Greyson, and D. James, eds., *The Handbook of Near-Death Experiences* (Santa Barbara, CA: Praeger/ABC-CLIO, 2009), 7.

23. Van Lommel, *Consciousness Beyond Life*, 132–33.

24. Miller, *Near-Death Experiences as Evidence*, 38–39.

25. Long and Perry, *Evidence of the Afterlife*, 6–7.

26. Long and Perry, *Evidence of the Afterlife*, 57–58.

27. Marvin J. Besteman and Lorilee Craker, *My Journey to Heaven: What I Saw and How It Changed My Life* (Grand Rapids: Baker, 2012), Kindle edition, location 12–14. Used by permission.

28. Van Lommel, *Consciousness Beyond Life*, 46.

29. "Hazeliene M NDE," NDERF.org, accessed August 8, 2019, http://www.nderf.org/NDERF/NDE_Experiences/hazeliene_m_nde.htm.

30. Besteman and Craker, *My Journey to Heaven*, 151.

31. Moody, *Life after Life*, 55.

32. Erlendur Haraldsson and Karlis Osis, *At the Hour of Death* (Guildford, Great Britain: White Crow Books, 1977), 184.

33. Dale Black and Ken Gire, *Flight to Heaven: A Plane Crash . . . A Lone Survivor . . . A Journey to Heaven—and Back* (Minneapolis: Bethany House, 2010), Kindle edition, locations 28–29, 98–106.

34. Richard Eby, *Caught Up into Paradise* (Old Tappan, NJ: Revell, 1978), 204–5.

35. Synopsis of Eben Alexander's NDE (including direct quotes) from Eben Alexander III, *Proof of Heaven* (New York: Simon & Schuster, 2012), Kindle edition, locations 8–9, 29–32, 38, 48–49, 143.

36. Ring and Cooper, *Mindsight*, 554–65.

37. Ring and Cooper, *Mindsight*, 27.

38. British Broadcasting Company, *The Day I Died*, http://top documentaryfilms.com/day-i-died/.

39. Black and Gire, *Flight to Heaven*, 100.

40. Long and Perry, *Evidence of the Afterlife*, 130.

41. Haraldsson and Osis, *At the Hour of Death*, 37.

42. Haraldsson and Osis, *At the Hour of Death*, 190–91.

43. Haraldsson and Osis, *At the Hour of Death*, 153.

44. Haraldsson and Osis, *At the Hour of Death*, 181.

45. Miller, *Near-Death Experiences as Evidence*, 83–85.

46. Moody, *Life after Life*, 78.

47. Faisal Malick, *10 Amazing Muslims Touched by God* (Shippensburg, PA: Destiny Image, 2012), Kindle edition, location 81.

48. Bodie Thoene and Samaa Habib, *Face to Face with Jesus: A Former Muslim's Extraordinary Journey to Heaven and Encounter with the God of Love* (Bloomington, MN: Chosen, 2014), Kindle edition, location 2157–65. Used by permission.

49. Miller, *Near-Death Experiences as Evidence*, 83–84.

50. Miller, *Near-Death Experiences as Evidence*, 86–87.

51. "Rene Hope Turner NDE," NDERF.org, accessed May 5, 2015, http://www.nderf.org/Experiences/1rene_hope_turner_nde.html.

52. Haraldsson and Osis, *At the Hour of Death*, 177.

53. Jenny Sharkey, *Clinically Dead—I've Seen Heaven and Hell* (Gospel Media, 2013), Kindle edition, location 25–31.

54. Thoene and Habib, *Face to Face with Jesus*, 176–80.

55. A. J. Ayer, "What I Saw When I Was Dead," *National Review* (October 14, 1988): 38–40.

56. Holden, Greyson, and James, eds., *Handbook of Near-Death Experiences*, 70; cited in Miller, *Near-Death Experiences as Evidence*, 170.

57. Van Lommel, *Consciousness Beyond Life*, 29–30.

58. From the transcript of John Burke's personal interview with Howard Storm.

59. From the transcript of John Burke's personal interview with Howard. The last two sentences in this paragraph are from Howard Storm, *My Descent into Death: A Second Chance at Life* (New York: Doubleday, 2005), 25.

60. From the transcript of John Burke's personal interview with Howard Storm. The last four sentences in this paragraph are from Storm, *My Descent into Death*, 26.

61. Moody, *Life after Life*, 92.

62. All quoted material about Howard Storm's NDE, aside from that which is cited with endnotes, is from the transcript of John Burke's personal interview with Howard Storm.

63. Long and Perry, *Evidence of the Afterlife*, 113.

64. From the transcript of an interview with Dr. Mary Neal by John Burke, October 2015.

65. Mary C. Neal, *To Heaven and Back: A Doctor's Extraordinary Account of Heaven, Angels, and Life Again: A True Story* (Colorado Springs: Waterbrook, 2012), Kindle edition, location 57.

66. Besteman and Craker, *My Journey to Heaven*, 75.

67. Black and Gire, *Flight to Heaven*, 109–10.

John Burke is the *New York Times* bestselling author of *Imagine Heaven, No Perfect People Allowed, Soul Revolution,* and *Unshockable Love*. As an international speaker and as a pastor, John has addressed hundreds of thousands of people in twenty countries on topics of leadership and spiritual growth. He lives in Austin, Texas. Learn more at WhatsAfterLife.com.

The **BESTSELLING BOOK**
That **STARTED** It All

NEW YORK TIMES BESTSELLER
Over 500,000 Copies Sold

IMAGINE HEAVEN

NEAR-DEATH EXPERIENCES,
GOD'S PROMISES,
AND THE EXHILARATING FUTURE
THAT AWAITS YOU

JOHN BURKE

FOREWORD BY DON PIPER
New York Times Bestselling Author of *90 Minutes in Heaven*

"In his engrossing book, my friend John Burke surveys the vast literature on NDEs, examining them in light of the Bible and showing how they can help us live with an eye on eternity."

—**LEE STROBEL**, bestselling author of
The Case for Christ and *The Case for Grace*

Visit ImagineHeaven.net to learn more!

BakerBooks
a division of Baker Publishing Group
www.BakerBooks.com

Available wherever books and ebooks are sold.